P9-ELR-087

GEORGE WASHINGTON

The Presidents of the United States

George Washington
1789–1797

John Adams
1797–1801

Thomas Jefferson
1801–1809

James Madison
1809–1817

James Monroe
1817–1825

John Quincy Adams
1825–1829

Andrew Jackson
1829–1837

Martin Van Buren
1837–1841

William Henry Harrison
1841

John Tyler
1841–1845

James Polk
1845–1849

Zachary Taylor
1849–1850

Millard Fillmore
1850–1853

Franklin Pierce
1853–1857

James Buchanan
1857–1861

Abraham Lincoln
1861–1865

Andrew Johnson
1865–1869

Ulysses S. Grant
1869–1877

Rutherford B. Hayes
1877–1881

James Garfield
1881

Chester Arthur
1881–1885

Grover Cleveland
1885–1889

Benjamin Harrison
1889–1893

Grover Cleveland
1893–1897

William McKinley
1897–1901

Theodore Roosevelt
1901–1909

William H. Taft
1909–1913

Woodrow Wilson
1913–1921

Warren Harding
1921–1923

Calvin Coolidge
1923–1929

Herbert Hoover
1929–1933

Franklin D. Roosevelt
1933–1945

Harry Truman
1945–1953

Dwight Eisenhower
1953–1961

John F. Kennedy
1961–1963

Lyndon Johnson
1963–1969

Richard Nixon
1969–1974

Gerald Ford
1974–1977

Jimmy Carter
1977–1981

Ronald Reagan
1981–1989

George H. W. Bush
1989–1993

William J. Clinton
1993–2001

George W. Bush
2001–present

GEORGE WASHINGTON

EDWARD F. DOLAN

Marshall Cavendish Benchmark
99 White Plains Road
Tarrytown, NY 10591-9001
www.marshallcavendish.us

All Internet addresses were correct at the time of printing.

Library of Congress Cataloging-in-Publication Data

Dolan, Edward F., 1924–
George Washington / by Edward F. Dolan.
p. cm. — (Presidents and their times)
Summary: "This series provides comprehensive information on the presidents of the United States and places each within his historical and cultural context. It also explores the formative events of his times and how he responds"—Provided by publisher.

Includes bibliographical references and index.

ISBN 978-0-7614-2427-7
1. Washington, George, 1732–1799—Juvenile literature. 2. Presidents—United States—Biography—Juvenile literature. I. Title. II. Series.
E312.66.D65 2008
973.4'1092—dc22
[B]

Editor: Christine Florie
Publisher: Michelle Bisson
Art Director: Anahid Hamparian
Series Designer: Alex Ferrari

Photo research by Connie Gardner

Cover photo by Gilbert Stuart/Museum of the City of New York/cc/CORBIS

The photographs in this book are used by permission and through the courtesy of: *Corbis:* Brooklyn Museum/Gilbert Stuart, 3, 83, 85 (R); CORBIS, 26, 74; Bettmann, 38, 45, 49, 55; *The Granger Collection:* 6, 9, 10, 12, 13, 14, 17, 20, 28, 29, 30, 32, 33, 36, 41, 47, 53, 57, 63, 65, 68, 70, 77, 80, 81, 84 (R), 85 (L); *North Wind Picture Archive:* 11, 15, 22, 39, 52, 60, 72, 84 (L); *Alamy:* North Wind, 24; *Art Resource:* The New York Public Library, 34; *Getty Images:* Hulton Archive, 43.

Printed in Malaysia

1 3 5 6 4 2

A VIRGINIA BOYHOOD IN A BRAVE NEW WORLD

$\mathcal{T}$he date was April 30, 1789. The place was New York City, outside a handsome building with tall windows and stately stone columns known as Federal Hall. Thousands of citizens gathered to catch a glimpse of a hero and witness a most momentous event—one that would surely be reported to successive generations for centuries to come.

Shortly after noon a procession appeared—first an honor guard, sworn to safely deliver the man who had played the most important role in their newly formed nation's recent struggle for freedom from its oppressive British masters. Beyond was a line of carriages, occupied first by those who had already taken positions in the newly organized government and then, finally and most inspiringly, by the beloved man himself, to whom all eyes were drawn. Behind his carriage, hundreds more citizens followed with reverence and anticipation.

The procession stopped about 200 yards short of the handsome building, and out stepped General George Washington. He was dressed in a dark brown suit, with a three-cornered hat, and a sword at his side. The honor guard lined either side of the street, and Washington walked between them. As he moved toward the hall, the crowd exploded into cheers. On the outside he seemed to exude both confidence and humility. Inside, however, he was experiencing a mixture of emotions—honor at being selected for the challenging post he was about to accept but also apprehension over whether he could, in fact, perform his duties to the satisfaction of his constituents. He knew the ways of a soldier, was familiar and comfortable on the fields of battle and in the company of other military men. But now he was being asked to devote his energies to an entirely different field—that of politics. He believed he knew little of it, but he accepted the responsibility out of a deep love for his country—one that was, in so many ways, just barely a country at all. It had a scant government, a shaky economy, few friends in the rest of the world, and citizens who had grown weary of hardship. They would be starting from scratch—and they were looking to this man to lead them to better days. Clearly there was a great deal of hard work ahead, and it could be done only by the wisest of men.

Washington stepped into Federal Hall and was introduced to the members of Congress. Then he went to the second floor and appeared on the balcony. Again the crowd displayed its affection through riotous applause. He bowed repeatedly in appreciation. Then a Bible was presented on a velvet pillow, and Washington set his right hand on it. The man who conducted the ceremony, Robert R. Livingston, was the chancellor of New York. And with the adoring crowd watching breathlessly, Livingston asked the hallowed question that would become so familiar to the succession of men in Washington's position:

Do you solemnly swear that you will faithfully execute the office of President of the United States and will, to the best of your abilities, preserve, protect, and defend the Constitution of the United States?

Washington answered in the affirmative and repeated the oath, closing with the four words that would also become a permanent part of the ritual: "So help me God."

With his vice president, John Adams, at his side, Washington then turned to his admirers, who offered another round of thunderous applause. And with this simple ceremony completed, George Washington became the first president of the United States.

BIRTH

By the time of George Washington's birth in 1732, the European colonization of North America was well under way. England, for example, had established thirteen separate colonies in North America, each with its own government and growing identity. But England also had heavy competition for North America's vast resources from some of its European neighbors—France, Spain, the Netherlands, and Sweden had all made claims on this exciting continent. In every sense the future United States was anything but united. By the time English settlers really began establishing themselves, France, Spain, and the Netherlands had already been there awhile, with France one day to claim territory from Canada all the way south to the coast of the Caribbean Sea.

One of the greatest advantages—and smartest strategic moves—of most of the competing nations was the forging of friendly relationships with the native peoples. They traded with them for goods and services, and they also taught the basic concepts of Christianity, which some Native Americans embraced.

History records that the English, for the most part, were not as kind as the other Europeans. Rather than search for unoccupied land and try to create some sort of harmony between themselves and the indigenous people, they often tried simply to force out the latter and claim prime farmland as their own. Fights between English colonists and Native Americans were common, and the better-equipped English often won. The English, as well

Many Europeans forged friendly alliances with the Native Americans by trading goods and services.

as other Europeans, also brought new illnesses with them, such as smallpox, which wiped out entire Native-American populations.

The governments of England's European neighbors grew increasingly concerned about their own interests, which were clearly being affected by England's negative presence. Tensions, therefore, ran high not only between the English settlers and the native people but also among all the European nations that wanted their newfound riches in North America to continue flowing smoothly. Little did the leaders of these nations realize that a man was being born in this hectic new frontier who would eventually change everything.

THE WASHINGTON FAMILY

On February 22, 1732, George Washington was born into a family of Virginia tobacco planters. His father, Augustine, also known as "Gus," was a tall, muscular, and friendly man.

George's mother, Mary, was Augustine's second wife; his first wife had died of a mysterious fever. With her marriage, Mary inherited a family of two growing sons—Lawrence and Augustine Jr. Then, in the next six years, she gave birth to six children—George, Betty, Samuel, John Augustine, Charles, and finally Mildred, who died in infancy.

Mary was twenty-three years old when she married Gus. The daughter of a local planter, she was known as a harsh woman who smoked a corncob pipe and loved horses, but seemed to have little love for George, rarely showing him deep affection. George returned her coolness, though he would dutifully provide her with money throughout his life.

The Washington family owned three homes in Virginia. All were tobacco plantations, with the first known as Wakefield. It was here that George was born. The two other homes were called Little Hunting Creek Plantation and Ferry Farm. Little Hunting Creek ran alongside the Potomac River, some 15 miles south of today's Washington, D.C. Gus's son Lawrence lived there for many years. He changed its name to Mount Vernon in honor of Edward Vernon, an old friend and vice admiral in the British navy. Ferry Farm lay alongside the Rappahannock River, opposite the village of Fredericksburg.

Mary Ball Washington, born in 1708, was the second wife of Augustine Washington and the mother of George.

Wakefield Plantation was the birthplace of George Washington. He lived there until he was three years old.

Altogether, the three plantations covered approximately 10,000 acres. At one time or another during his young years, George lived on all three properties. With their 10,000 acres the Washingtons were a prosperous family. But they were far from rich when compared with some of their neighbors. One neighbor, Thomas Lord Fairfax, held a stunning five million acres. When George reached his teens, Lord Fairfax would play an important role in his life.

A Virginia Boyhood

Life was busy for George from his earliest years. Much of his time was spent in the family fields, learning the skills of farming that he would use as an adult. In addition to raising tobacco, his family—as did all other colonial families—produced most of what they

THE WASHINGTONS: TOBACCO PLANTERS

Most Americans remember George Washington as a soldier and as our nation's first president. While he found lasting fame in these two tasks, he earned his living for most of his life as a tobacco planter and—to provide his family and workers with the everyday necessities of life—as a farmer.

The Washington family's history in America began in 1657, when George's great-grandfather John left his home in southern England, sailed to America, and settled in Virginia. He acquired his first property on marrying Anne Pope, the daughter of a neighboring tobacco planter. He became a prosperous landowner and tobacco farmer, along the way earning the name "town taker" from the local Native Americans, not because of any military prowess but because they accused him of cheating them out of their land. Then his sons Lawrence and John Jr. added to the acreage. Finally Lawrence's son Gus completed the family purchases.

Tobacco gave the Washington family and many other Virginia families their principal livelihood. By the time of George's birth, it had become a major source of wealth for the people of the Virginia colony that the king of England would want shared with the motherland.

needed for survival. The crops included apples, vegetables, and grains, while the livestock ranged from chickens and cows for food to horses for transportation.

But life was not all work for the boy. There was time for swimming, hunting game, exploring the surrounding countryside, and watching the river traffic that sailed past the three family homes. Of his many pastimes, however, the young Virginian's favorite was horseback riding. He became an especially skilled rider early—and remained skilled until, in his advanced age, he no longer had the dexterity to swing into the saddle. As horsemanship was an important skill in those days, his considerable abilities served him well in his later years, first as a military commander and then as an honored and admired public figure. Thomas Jefferson even remembered him as "the best horseman of his age, and the most graceful figure that could be seen on horseback."

In the midst of all these activities, George received his earliest education, first at home from a local man hired by Gus and then in a village school. Very little is known of the boy's schoolwork, though he left behind a number of notebooks showing that he studied Latin, geography, history, and mathematics. They also show that he quickly developed a very legible and graceful handwriting. Historians who later studied the

As a boy, George received his education at a village school much like this one.

notes, letters, and speeches that he wrote throughout his long public life were grateful for his penmanship.

In those early years, however, his fine handwriting was offset by his atrocious spelling, which included such errors as *blew* for *blue* and *oyl* for *oil*. Fortunately the problem began to disappear as he grew older and decided to use a dictionary while writing.

A problem concerning his education gave George great disappointment early in life.

Young George looked up to his older half brother and mentor, Lawrence (above).

His two half brothers—Lawrence and Augustine Jr.—had been sent to England as young men and had completed their educations there. Of the two, George especially admired Lawrence, who was fourteen years his senior. He hoped to be just like Lawrence one day, respected for his intelligence and fine manners. And so, knowing that his father planned the same schooling for him, he was eagerly looking forward to the coming English journey.

But in 1743, when he was eleven, George's life was turned upside down. Gus suffered a sudden and fatal illness. The loss was a heartbreaking one for George, with its pain made even worse when Gus's property was divided among his survivors. In keeping with the custom of the day, the greatest share, consisting of two homes, went to his two oldest sons—Mount Vernon to Lawrence and Wakefield to Augustine Jr. Smaller gifts went to Mary and her children, with George receiving Ferry Farm.

The inheritance was a disappointment for the youngster. It provided far too little money to finance a stay in England. The dream of a fine British education and all that it promised for his future suddenly evaporated, leaving George with no idea of what life would hold for him. He was left, however, with the determination to become as fine and respected a gentleman as his half brother Lawrence.

The next years were made even more difficult for George by his mother. They lived together at Ferry Farm, with Mary continuing to be distant and unloving, never saying a complimentary thing about her son—a silence that would persist until her death, in 1789, a short time after he became the nation's first president. The time spent with Mary was so miserable for the young Virginian that he constantly invented excuses to escape to Mount Vernon for visits.

A New Life

George was always welcomed at Mount Vernon by Lawrence— whom a neighbor said George was soon calling "my best friend"—with his visits growing more frequent and lasting ever longer. Finally, keenly aware of the boy's unhappiness, Lawrence invited him to come live at Mount Vernon permanently, an invitation that the fourteen-year-old quickly accepted. A short time later the two were joined by Anne Fairfax, when she and Lawrence were married. Her father was the owner of the nearby Belvoir plantation.

Now came happy years for young George. His days at Mount Vernon were occupied with varied activities. He rode horses, participated in fox hunts with neighbors, learned to play card games,

George enjoyed his time at Mount Vernon, where he participated in fox hunts and other activities.

developed a lifelong taste for the theater, and took dancing and fencing lessons. He became well known for his dancing skills—and for his love of fashionable clothes. It was a love that was seen early, when he designed a coat for himself. In his instructions to the tailor he specified the number and placement of the buttons, plus the width of the lapels.

The years at Mount Vernon also witnessed George's physical growth. With auburn hair and blue eyes, he was on his way to reaching a height of 6 feet 2.5 inches—more than a half-foot taller than the average man of the 1700s. He would soon have broad shoulders, long arms and legs, and extremely large hands. He was becoming admired among his friends for his physical strength and for his claim—which no one seems to have doubted—that he once threw a rock up to the Natural Bridge in the Shenandoah Valley, a 215-foot-high rock arch.

In spite of the many good graces that would eventually earn him the adoration of thousands of his fellow Americans, he displayed a temper in his early years that would follow him through life. When he was just sixteen, it caused Thomas Lord Fairfax to remark, "I wish I could say he governs his temper." Later it showed itself when his officers failed him during the Revolution that would change the course of America forever, prompting Alexander Hamilton to recall, perhaps sarcastically, that the general was not "remarkable . . . for delicacy nor for good temper." It arose once during his presidency, when he came upon press reports that he thought unfairly criticized his work.

George's temper and the need to control it may well have been among the reasons for a gift that he received in his teens from his brother Lawrence. It was a popular booklet containing a number of rules for good behavior, 110 in all, that had first been published in 1595. It had then been expanded several times over the decades and had appeared under various titles in Europe, among them *Youths Behaviour*, or *Decency in Conversation among Men*. The book offered such advice as

Use no reproachful language against any one, neither curse nor revile.
Speak not evil of the absent for it is unjust.
Wear not your clothes foul [or] ripped or dirty, but see that they be brushed once every day at least . . .

Lawrence obviously thought the rules were especially important for anyone who wished to be successful in his business and personal life. George just as obviously agreed with his brother and, in an effort never to forget them, painstakingly wrote them into a notebook.

While filling his notebook with the rules, George also began a study that would soon lead to a career. He had become interested in surveying—the work of measuring and mapping land areas—while watching a number of surveyors at work near Mount Vernon. Sensing that the knowledge of surveying would be a great help to him as a landowner, he hunted down a set of surveying instruments once owned by his father and began to train himself by measuring sections of the nearby farmlands and a small forest. It was also valuable knowledge because so much of North America was still awaiting settlement and would eventually be divided among the thousands of new settlers who were pouring in from across the sea with each passing year.

In the midst of this study George Washington's young life took a sudden turn that led him to adventure, soldiering, and along the way, heartbreak.

FIRST ADVENTURES AS WAR BEGINS

Two

$\mathcal{B}$y the mid-1700s tension between the English and the French were heading toward the boiling point. The English colonies were growing at an ever-quickening pace in terms of both economy and population. Each colony had built a relatively sturdy government, discovered a resource or two (or more) that enabled it to earn tremendous profits, and saw a growing immigration from its homeland as more and more settlers came in search of new lives. It seemed as though the English colonies were becoming the dominant force in North America.

During the mid-1700s the English colonies grew at a fast pace as new settlers arrived, expanding the economy with trade and crafts.

The colonists did not necessarily see it this way, however. The French still claimed the great bulk of the land and made no secret that they wanted even more—as much as possible, in fact. But the French had lost a great deal of power and prestige throughout the world in 1713 with a treaty that would become known as the Peace of Utrecht, which ended a series of inter-European conflicts. Through this multinational agreement, the influence of the great European countries changed radically, and as a result, the French gave up much of the North American land they had gained in exchange for smaller prizes, such as control over much of the profitable sugar trade in the West Indian islands.

This sudden and newfound English domination very naturally left a bad taste in France's mouth, and the still-formidable nation decided that, peace treaty or not, it wasn't going to give up its North American territories quite so easily. The French continued trading with the natives and building military outposts in strategic locations. This put a great strain on their homeland, as the government of France had to support the effort with military resources and direct cash payouts. But France's determination and stubbornness was, perhaps, greater than its common sense. As France continued squabbling with England over who owned what, it seemed that yet another conflict between the two was approaching. No one could have predicted that a young and anonymous Virginia youth named George Washington would almost single-handedly light the fuse.

EARLY WORK

The first of the many adventures that marked Washington's life began when he was only fifteen years old. It was then that he met a visiting relative of Lawrence Washington's wife, Anne. The visitor was Thomas Lord Fairfax, a cousin of Anne's father.

They met when George accompanied Lawrence and Anne to a dinner at Belvoir, the Fairfax plantation. Lord Fairfax was staying there while on a trip from England in the hope of selling portions of a massive property that he owned in Virginia. It covered more than five million acres.

Lord Fairfax's land lay in Virginia's distant Shenandoah Valley. It had never been cultivated for planting, and now, before it could be divided into parcels and sold, it needed to be surveyed. Fairfax hired a team of surveyors for the job. Then he invited a delighted young George to join the group. Fairfax issued the invitation because George had impressed him deeply with his enthusiasm for surveying, his fine manners, and his superb horsemanship.

The now-sixteen-year-old boy was soon hiking into the wilderness. It was an experience that would no doubt serve him well in years to come when, as a military commander, he had to fight several key battles in the woodlands of his home territory—and against an army that was not as familiar as he with such an environment.

Tucked away among his gear was a diary that he had

By the time George Washington was sixteen, he was working as a land surveyor for Thomas Lord Fairfax.

purchased to record his first trip away from home. With it he began a lifelong habit of writing daily of his experiences.

In that first diary he wrote a fascinating account of his life on the trail. Whenever possible, the travelers stayed the night at small cabins along the way, paying their owners for their hospitality. In one early entry George wrote of undressing and climbing into bed while his companions curled up on the floor, fully dressed. Then he found the bed

> . . . to be nothing but a Little Straw—matted together without Sheets or anything else but only one thread Bear blanket with double its weight of Vermin such as Lice, Fleas &. I was glad to get up . . . I put on my Clothes and lay as my Companions. Had we not been very tired I am sure we should not have slep'd much that night. I made a Promise not to Sleep so from that time forward, chusing rather to sleep in ye open Air before a fire . . . .

During the next few days the party moved through a heavy rain toward the Fairfax property. They hiked overland, paddled canoes along rivers, and shot wild game for their meals. On a trip marked by memorable adventures, perhaps the most memorable came when they met a band of Native Americans who entertained them with a war dance performed to the rhythm of a deerskin drum.

The work at the survey site took thirty days in early 1748. They were among the most valuable in sixteen-year-old George's life. They set him on the road to becoming a master surveyor and enabled him, in the next three years, to conduct 190 surveys. Later in 1748 he was named the assistant surveyor for his county, Fairfax. From 1749 to 1751 he served as its chief surveyor, and it is likely he would have continued in this profession and perhaps even been quite successful at it. But then tragedy struck.

For some twenty years George's beloved brother Lawrence had suffered from tuberculosis, with the illness steadily worsening until it finally claimed his life in 1752. Lawrence's death led to two significant developments in George's life. The first concerned Mount Vernon. The estate passed to Anne as Lawrence's widow, but she moved away after a time, when she remarried and went to live at her new husband's distant estate. George remained at Mount Vernon by himself, renting it from Anne until her death a few years later. He then became the sole owner of the home that he would occupy for the rest of his days.

After Lawrence Washington died, his rank in the Virginia militia was passed on to his half brother George (above).

The second development altered the direction of his life—plus that of his entire country. For years Lawrence had served in the Virginia militia. In that time he had risen to the rank of major and had sparked George's interest in soldiering. Governor Robert Dinwiddie of Virginia, knowing of that interest, now passed Lawrence's rank to George. At age twenty-one George began a military career that would eventually see him in command of all the colonial troops struggling to give birth to the United States.

COLONIAL BATTLES IN OHIO

Soon after his appointment as a major in the militia Washington

THE YOUNG SOLDIER

Though George Washington's military career began at age twenty-one, his interest in soldiering may well have dated back to his early childhood. According to a story told about him, his soldiering life began when he was just a boy and his father gave him a toy sword. The sword instantly became a favorite plaything and was with him daily as he fought imaginary battles, defeating his enemies and capturing battlefield prizes.

It is unknown whether this story is true or imagined, but if true in any part, it reveals an early love for soldiering that was to follow Washington through his life, joining farming, tobacco planting, and politics as major endeavors, giving him some of his greatest moments.

Because there were no military schools in the colonies, Lawrence took on the job of giving George his early military training. George was soon assisted by several militia officers who were Lawrence's closest friends and frequent guests at Mount Vernon. Together they coached their young charge in fencing, handling of arms, use of artillery, mapmaking and map reading, battle tactics, and leadership skills. On top of all else they provided the stories of militia adventure that were so often told around the dining table, stories sure to fire a youngster's imagination and ambition.

was sent on the first of four military missions to the Virginia frontier. In 1753 Governor Dinwiddie ordered him and three companions west 500 miles to the Ohio Valley. The region had long been a source of dispute between England and France, with each wanting to gain control of it for its natural riches. Washington was now to check on reports that French troops

George Washington's mission into the Ohio Valley in 1753 proved his exemplary service to the militia.

were entering the valley from Canada and building three forts there. If so, he was to tell them that they were trespassing and were to leave immediately.

In December, near Lake Erie, Washington located the first of the forts and delivered the message. It was coldly rejected by the French commander, leaving Washington and his companions to hike home through a blinding snowstorm.

For his exemplary service the young officer was promoted to lieutenant colonel. Then Dinwiddie ordered him back to the Ohio Valley, now with 150 troops and instructions to stall the French advances by building a fort on the site of present-day Pittsburgh, Pennsylvania. But upon nearing his goal, Washington received word that the French had already built a post there, naming it Fort Duquesne. The French then sent out a force to stop Washington and his men from advancing.

Washington brought his troops to a halt and had them piece together a makeshift fortification, which he christened Fort Necessity. When the French approached, he moved forward from the tiny installation and positioned his troops for an ambush. During this time he ordered his men to begin firing—an order that many would later call the opening shots of the French and Indian Wars. In a report that he later wrote about the next moments, he recalled, "I heard the bullets whistle and, believe me, there is something charming in the sound."

Washington's strategy worked for a time, but facing far superior numbers, his troops were eventually driven back into Necessity. Finally, on July 3, 1754, a daylong battle in a violent storm cost Washington half of his troops and left him with no choice but to surrender to the enemy.

The French then said that Washington and his troops would be freed if he promised not to build a fort in the area for a year. With many of his men wounded and in need of medical help, the young lieutenant colonel reluctantly nodded and led the way back to Virginia. Washington was greeted not as a fail-ure, however, but as a hero and, in March 1755, was promoted to the rank of colonel. At the same time, at age twenty-three, he was named aide-de-camp to British Major General Edward

By 1755 Washington was promoted to colonel in the Virginia militia. He was twenty-three years old.

Braddock, who had just arrived in the colony.

Immediately on his arrival, Braddock set out for Fort Duquesne with two of his own regiments, plus militiamen from the British colonies of Virginia, Maryland, and the Carolinas. His force totaled some 2,400 men. Also on the march were a number of Native-American warriors who supported the British. Colonel George Washington was at his side, as a volunteer aide, assisting the general with various duties.

On July 9, as the troops neared Duquesne, they entered a wooded area and were ambushed by some 850 French, Canadian, and Native-American fighters. Gunfire erupted from the thick underbrush and from behind trees and rocks. All along the line of the march, British **redcoats** and colonial militiamen began pitching forward on their faces.

At first panic erupted among the British. Trained for open-field warfare, they were strangers to an ambush. But they rallied and drove off the French, only to have the enemy strike with fresh fire. Again, panic spread throughout the British ranks. Some turned and fled. Many began firing blindly and cutting down their own men.

The Virginians, too, were stunned by the sudden onslaught. But with their knowledge of Native American fighting techniques, they took cover and fought successfully under Washington's direction after most of the British officers were wounded. Within minutes, though, two horses were shot out from under Washington, and his uniform was ripped by four musket balls. In the same moments General Braddock fell when a musket ball struck one lung, killing him.

General Braddock was one of the nine hundred British and colonists who were killed or wounded in the fighting. Now, with Washington leading, the battered troops struggled home. The young officer was immediately hailed as a hero and was named commander of all militia forces in Virginia. A tremendous honor for a man of twenty-three, it won him the command of troops who were building a string of forts along the colony's border between 1755 and 1757.

After leading troops during the French and Indian Wars, Washington was named commander of all Virginia's militia forces.

George Washington raises his hat to the British flag over Fort Duquesne in November 1758.

In 1758, on his fourth trip westward, Washington accompanied a British force under General John Forbes as it finally captured and claimed Fort Duquesne for good. The journey marked Washington's last military activity for more than seventeen years. After being awarded the honorary rank of brigadier general, he resigned from the militia and looked forward to a new life as a successful plantation owner. It was a life he would spend for the coming decade as the husband of a young woman named Martha Dandridge Custis, but it was also one that he would not be able to enjoy for long. As America continued along its road to freedom and independence, evolution would quickly turn into revolution, and George Washington would find himself in the middle of it.

THE MARCH TO REVOLUTION

Three

$\mathcal{T}$he French and Indian Wars would become the last of four struggles waged in the Old World and New World by France, Great Britain, and other European nations between 1689 and 1763. For Britain and France there was a simple question: which of the two would emerge as the major power on the North American continent?

The first three conflicts were known as King William's War (1689–96), Queen Anne's War (1700–13), and King George's War (1744–48). The fourth was fought from 1754 to 1763 and was called by two names—the French and Indian Wars in America and the Seven Years' War in Europe. In time the name of the American conflict was made to embrace all four.

In the French and Indian Wars both France and Britain employed the braves of the surrounding tribes as warriors. Among those who fought for the British were the Chickasaw, the Creek, and the Cherokee, while those who supported the French included the Ottawa, the Shawnee, and the Seneca. Behind the Native American willingness to take part in a "white man's war" was the hope that the fighting would drive one or the other of the two outsiders—or both—from the New World.

When the fighting began, both France and Great Britain were major landholders in the Americas. When the fighting ended, France would lose the bulk of its New World holdings to Britain—Canada and all the possessions east of the Mississippi

River and south to the outskirts of the city of New Orleans. Also in British hands was the former Spanish possession that would one day become the state of Florida.

PEACE AND CONTENTMENT—FOR A WHILE

When she came to Mount Vernon as a bride, Martha Washington was twenty-seven years old, the same age as George, and the widow of a wealthy plantation owner named Daniel Parke Custis. She brought with her two small children, Jacky and Patsy.

Martha was an energetic woman, blessed with a goodly share of common sense. Though not beautiful, she was attractive and, physically, the exact opposite of her new husband. George now stood 6 feet 2.5 inches tall—a towering height for a man of his day—while Martha managed to reach just over 5 feet. Plump and dainty, she was good-humored in contrast to her husband, who had a serious and dignified manner.

As George Washington's wife, Martha was most concerned about the comfort and happiness of her family.

George courted Martha for just a short while and then suddenly appeared at the Custis plantation one day in 1758, proposed marriage, and was accepted. The proposal was followed by a wedding on January 6, 1759.

The couple, along with Martha's two children, immediately moved into Mount Vernon. After his absences, due mostly to his first military service, Washington found the plantation sadly neglected. He began rebuilding the home itself and returning the fields to full flower. He was determined to make Mount Vernon one of the grandest plantations in the colony. Even though he had not enjoyed the advantages of an English education, he could still build a home that would mark him as a true gentleman of wealth.

When Washington lived at Mount Vernon, it consisted of five farms spread over 8,000 acres. The farm where he and his family lived was called Mansion House Farm (above).

The efforts of the couple steadily bore fruit. A new and enlarged main house took shape over the years. The surrounding fields were soon yielding the crops needed for daily sustenance, plus tobacco and wheat. What's more, fish caught in the nearby Potomac River could be exported to England. Washington also used his land for experiments in crop rotation and plowing.

Also tending to Mount Vernon were dozens of workers who provided the plantation with practically all that it needed to support its people. Among them were orchardists, farmers, fishermen, and carpenters. Over the years they were joined by some three hundred or more slaves.

Washington had a reputation for treating his slaves fairly and with care but doing little more for them than most other planters.

He housed them in small cabins, fed and clothed them, employed a doctor to treat their ills, and tried never to separate family members in slave trades. In later years he would come to detest the very idea of slavery, once writing that he wished it could be "abolished by slow, sure, and imperceptible degrees." This dislike was fostered by such friends as the Marquis de Lafayette, the young French nobleman who served under him in the Revolutionary War. In his will Washington called for half of his slaves to be freed after his death. Martha freed them all in 1800, two years before her death and one year after her husband's.

Daily life for the young Washington consisted mainly of long hours in the saddle as he supervised the work in his fields. But life

George Washington found time away from the fields of his farm to socialize with friends and neighbors.

also held more than work for him. Mount Vernon was almost always crowded with guests—friends and relatives who were visiting or passing through to other destinations. Because there were few inns in which travelers could stay the night, it was customary for the surrounding homes to welcome them. Washington enjoyed the guests, parties, and picnics. Most of all he liked dancing, an art that he learned when, at age fifteen, he began attending a nearby dancing school. It was an activity that he would treasure into his final years.

In the House of Burgesses

In 1759, as the French and Indian Wars raged throughout North America, Washington was elected to the Virginia House of Burgesses, a body of citizens who assisted the Virginia governor in developing laws for the colony.

During his time in Burgesses, Washington earned the reputation of being a serious, quiet legislator. A fellow member, Thomas Jefferson, would one day write his recollections of Washington and another unforgettable American, the Pennsylvanian Benjamin Franklin:

I never heard either of them speak for ten minutes at a time, not to any but the main point which was to decide the question. They laid their shoulders to the great points, knowing that the little ones would follow of themselves.

Washington served in Burgesses from 1759 until 1775, resigning his post when he took command of the American forces in the Revolutionary War. From then on he did not represent just one colony but all thirteen.

His first years with Burgesses were quiet ones for Washington, who used them to learn about lawmaking. But the next years brought mounting friction between the colonies and Great Britain, at last putting them sharply at odds with each other. Up to this point British royalty paid relatively little attention to the North American colonies, and a harmonious and mutually beneficial relationship existed between them. They traded for various goods, and the colonists dutifully paid their taxes and other homage to their homeland in good faith while the leadership in London more or less maintained a policy of noninterference.

The trouble began in 1763, when Britain's newly crowned King George III looked at the costs of the just-ended French and Indian Wars and realized that the mother country had spent a fortune to protect its American colonies. It was a debt, he insisted, that the colonies must repay.

King George III was committed to taxing the American colonies, which ultimately led to the American Revolution and independence in 1776.

THE ROAD TO REVOLUTION

The king began covering his country's wartime debts by ordering the colonies to obey what were called the Navigation Acts. These had been enacted decades earlier by the British Parliament to help England profit from the growing trade between its colonies and various nations in South America and Europe. They dictated that colonial cargo ships, when sailing to foreign ports, must go through British ports first and pay custom fees.

The colonists had always resented the acts, but they had never actively rebelled against them. They had simply ignored the lot and built a highly profitable smuggling trade. The British government, facing military problems elsewhere, had turned a blind eye on the situation.

But now, in 1763, the king demanded that the acts be strictly enforced. At sea British warships began stopping colonial vessels for searches and the payment of fees. On land British officials charged into homes without search warrants—often at night—to sniff out goods about to be smuggled. Immediately the colonists cried that their right to privacy was being violated.

Another angry cry echoed through the colonies in 1763 when the news arrived that colonial businesses must now pay tariffs on a growing number of English products—everything from clothing and housewares to tools. Then in 1765 came the hated Stamp Act. It required the colonists to pay a tax on various printed items they used, among them letters, newspapers, and even playing cards. The Stamp Act enraged the public. Furious, the colonists claimed that the king had no right to tax them directly, because they had no representatives in the British Parliament.

Because of the American outrage the British government canceled the Stamp Act in 1766. Its repeal triggered celebrations throughout the colonies. But they soon ended with Parliament's passage of new measures—called the Townshend Acts—that imposed taxes on a string of goods vital to daily colonial life. Among them were lead, paper, paint, glass, and tea.

AMERICANS!
BEAR IN REMEMBRANCE
The HORRID MASSACRE!
Perpetrated in King-ftreet, Boston,
New-England.
On the Evening of March the Fifth, 1770.
When FIVE of your fellow countrymen,
GRAY, MAVERICK, CALDWELL, ATTUCKS,
and CARR,
Lay wallowing in their Gore!
Being *bafely*, and moft *inhumanly*
MURDERED!
And SIX others badly WOUNDED!
By a Party of the XXIXth Regiment,
Under the command of Capt. Tho. Prefton.
REMEMBER!
That Two of the MURDERERS
Were convicted of MANSLAUGHTER!
By a Jury, of whom I fhall fay
NOTHING,
Branded in the hand!
And *difmiffed*,
The others were ACQUITTED,
And their Captain .PENSIONED!
Alfo,
BEAR IN REMEMBRANCE
That on the 22d Day of February, 1770
The infamous
EBENEZER RICHARDSON, Informer,
And tool to Minifterial hirelings,
Moft *barbaroufly*
MURDERED
CHRISTOPHER SEIDER,
An innocent youth!
Of which crime he was found guilty
By his Country
On Friday April 20th, 1770;
But remained *Unfentenced*
On Saturday the 22d Day of February, 1772.
When the GRAND INQUEST
For Suffolk county,
Were informed, at requeft,
By the Judges of the Superior Court,
That EBENEZER RICHARDSON'S *Cafe*
Then lay before his MAJESTY.
Therefore faid Richardfon

*Part of a handbill distributed in
1770 by the Committees of
Correspondence describes the
Boston Massacre.*

Angry anti-Townshend demonstrations erupted everywhere, with the worst occurring in the Massachusetts Bay Colony. In the city of Boston on March 5, 1770, British troops fired on a group of rock-throwing demonstrators, killing four or five and injuring several. Known as the Boston Massacre, the incident was broadcast throughout the colonies by the Committees of Correspondence.

By sad coincidence the Boston Massacre occurred on the very day that Parliament repealed all the tariffs except one. King George refused to cancel the tax on tea. His refusal, he said, would show the colonists that he would not bend to their every wish.

The colonists at first peacefully boycotted English tea, and George Washington, whose resentment of Britain's increasing greed and oppression grew almost daily, fully supported this boycott. Colonists quietly bought tea smuggled in from the West Indies for three years. But this era of subtle defiance ended in Boston Harbor on the night of December 16, 1773. It was then that a number of townspeople disguised as Native Americans crowded aboard three tea-carrying ships from England and pitched their cargoes overboard, sending 342 tea cases into the water. Word of the attack spread everywhere, and the event earned a nickname, the Boston Tea Party.

The ships in Boston were not alone in being attacked. Tea-carrying ships in five other cities also faced angry receptions in the next days. In New York, for example, one had its tea dumped into the East River. Philadelphia permitted cargo to be unloaded but then left it to rot at dockside.

News of the Tea Party was met with mixed feelings through-out the colonies. Many colonists applauded what Boston had

On December 16, 1773, Boston townspeople, dressed as Native Americans, destroyed tea shipments from England in protest of King George's tea tax.

done, but just as many condemned the night's work as an act of vandalism. In Britain a furious King George insisted that the colonists be punished. In 1774 he had Parliament enact what the colonists christened the Intolerable Acts.

There were five acts in all, with four of them aimed at Massachusetts. The first dictated that the port of Boston would be closed until the people of the city paid for the lost tea.

With the second, the government in London deprived the Massachusetts people of any voice in the political affairs of their colony. All officials were to be appointed by King George rather than by local election. Town meetings could be held only if permitted by the colony's governor.

According to the third any colonial official or British soldier who was charged with killing someone in the line of duty could now be sent to England for trial. This measure enraged the colonists, who believed that, once in England, the accused would be judged innocent and set free. This law applied to all the colonies, not just to Massachusetts.

The fourth Intolerable Act was known as the Quartering Act. It required that people everywhere in the colonies allow their public buildings, inns, and even private homes to be used to house British troops. The law was borne of the fear that the unrest caused by the Boston Tea Party would trigger further trouble and would require that an increased military force be brought in from England.

The fifth of the Intolerable Acts enabled the British government to add the sprawling and rich land between the Ohio River and the Great Lakes to the Canadian province of Quebec. Some colonists considered this a punishment because it involved land wanted for settlement by Virginia, New York, Connecticut, and Massachusetts.

The Colonial Population: Mid-1770s

At the time of the Revolutionary War more than two million settlers were living in the thirteen colonies, with the greatest number being English speaking and of English, Irish, Welsh, or Scottish descent.

Though the English-speaking population contributed a major share of the revolutionary fighters, they were joined by settlers of Dutch, French, German, Swedish, and Swiss descent. In all, including more than 65,000 black slaves, almost 40 percent of the people of British colonial America were of non-English origin.

Though about 90 percent of the colonists lived in rural areas, the major population centers in the 1770s were Philadelphia (below), with the largest population; New York; Boston; and Charleston. The diversity of the population could best be seen in Philadelphia, where the street signs were printed in both English and German.

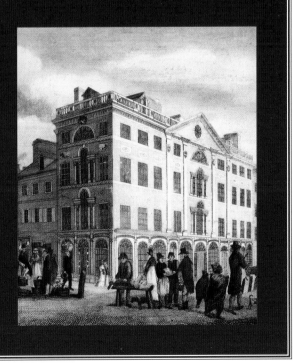

The colonies boasting the greatest number of people in 1775 were, in descending order, Virginia, Massachusetts, Pennsylvania, Maryland, and North Carolina.

The anger triggered by the Intolerable Acts led to one of the most famous statements in American history. It came from Patrick Henry during a speech to his fellow members of the Virginia legislature:

Is life so dear and peace so sweet as to be purchased at the price of chains and slavery? Forbid it, Almighty God! I know not what course others may take, but, as for me, give me liberty or give me death!

Most colonists viewed the Intolerable Acts as brutally unfair. Steps had to be taken to be rid of them. But the opinions on what should be done were sharply divided. On one side were people who felt that strong requests to England for fair treatment were all that were needed. On the other were those who were beginning to murmur of the need for rebellion—and among them was George Washington.

A CONTINENTAL CONGRESS

The murmur would grow in intensity as time passed. But in 1774 most colonists wanted only fair treatment. To seek that treatment, fifty-five delegates from twelve of the thirteen colonies (Georgia was absent) met in Philadelphia from September 5 to October 26, 1774, for what they called a continental congress (in time, it would be called the First Continental Congress). They discussed their problems with London and then sent the king a letter titled "A Declaration of Rights and Grievances."

In it the delegates held that Parliament had no right to tax the colonies because there were no American representatives in Parliament. Only the colonists had the right to tax their fellow citizens. The declaration then petitioned the king to correct the wrongs being done to his American subjects. The request was politely worded, since most of the delegates, though infuriated, were still loyal to the motherland and respectful of the monarch.

Once the request was written, the delegates agreed to meet again soon for a Second Continental Congress and then returned home. There, they learned that their plea had suffered the insult of being ignored. The king's silence took the colonies—and George Washington—a step closer to an angry break.

The First Continental Congress sent a signed letter to King George III listing colonial grievances against Britain and included a declaration of the rights of the colonies. This page shows the delegates' signatures.

WASHINGTON'S GROWING INVOLVEMENT

In his early years with Burgesses, Washington played little or no part in the criticisms leveled at the Crown, always sitting quietly and listening to the group's debates. But as time passed and he heard outcries against British wrongs such as Patrick Henry's "Give me liberty or give me death" speech, he found it increasingly difficult, and then impossible, to ignore the colonial anger.

He was especially outraged at the way the Crown and Parliament were trampling on the rights of the people of Boston and all the colonies. In 1768, at age thirty-six, he told a friend that he would shoulder his musket whenever his country called for his help. Soon thereafter he admitted that he fully supported the idea of warfare if England continued its mistreatment of the colonists. He added that no man should shun the idea of using firearms to defend his country's liberty.

In 1769 he joined his fellow members in Burgesses when they opposed the early tariff on clothing. As one, they swore to ban all arriving British apparel for both men and women. Washington joined the boycott, but as a lifelong admirer of stylish outfits, he soon grew tired of repeatedly wearing his old clothes and decided to ignore the ban. In time he was joined by an increasing number of well-to-do colonists, and the ban was eventually dropped.

In July 1774 Washington attended a meeting of Burgesses and voted to designate Philadelphia as the site for the First Continental Congress. He then joined his fellow Virginians in selecting seven delegates to represent the colony at the Congress. He was the third of the seven chosen.

Throughout the congressional meetings Washington listened to the speeches and the debate, met the members of the various delegations, and impressed them with his calm manner and the clarity of his thinking when discussing the colonists' complaints.

When Congress adjourned on October 26, 1774, Washington returned home. Within six months he would again be in Philadelphia, this time for the Second Continental Congress. By then the first blood had been spilled in the American Revolution, and he was about to step into the pages of U.S. history.

THE REVOLUTIONARY YEARS: 1775–1783

Washington arrived in Philadelphia in early May 1775 for the Second Continental Congress. The city crackled with the talk of war with England, a war that was looming much because of the unruly behavior of colonists in Massachusetts.

The latest conflict in Massachusetts erupted when General Thomas Gage, the British commander in Boston, sent seven hundred men to the nearby village of Concord, where a rebel group was said to be amassing arms.

The British departed at night on April 18, 1775. They had hoped to march in secret, only to find that the colonists had learned of the move and had gathered at two places to stop them, the village of Lexington and Concord itself.

American colonists and British redcoats exchange fire at the Battle of Lexington.

At dawn there was the rattle of musketry when the British met more than seventy colonists at Lexington. Eight colonists lost their lives, and ten fell wounded. By midmorning the redcoats reached Concord and found no sign of hidden arms. But on beginning their return to Boston, they did find a group of armed Concord patriots. Then came bursts of gunfire that took the lives of two colonists and six British.

Now fighting raged for hours as the British struggled back to Boston with the colonists pursuing and constantly firing at them. The chase finally ended at dusk. By then more than 250 redcoats had been killed or wounded.

PREPARING FOR WAR: 1775

On arriving in Philadelphia several weeks later, Washington found many in the city almost eager for revolution. He also found that men throughout the colonies had already gone beyond mere talk—some 14,000 had flooded into Boston and entrenched themselves in the hills ringing the city. Now, as the Continental Congress began its work at Philadelphia, they waited for General Gage to come out and fight. He refused to budge. He was quietly waiting while a message traveled across the Atlantic Ocean to London. It contained his request for 4,500 reinforcements, which would bring his forces to a total of 8,000. Once they arrived, he would take action.

In the meantime the Continental Congress prepared for war. The delegates first formed committees to study military planning. Then they established the Continental Army. It would consist of the long-standing militia units and a small volunteer force. The volunteers would enlist for two years of service.

Finally the delegates set about selecting the army's commander-in-chief. Several men, all fine militia leaders, were

George Washington took command of the Continental Army after being chosen by the delegates of the Continental Congress.

considered. When the final vote came on June 15, 1775, the post went to George Washington. With it went a salary that he refused, asking only that his expenses be repaid.

The forty-three-year-old Virginian modestly expressed surprise that he had been selected. But there was no reason for surprise. His service with General Braddock had won him lasting fame throughout the colonies. Further, everyone attending the Congress could see how much he wanted to serve in some way. He made his desire known by constantly wearing his militia uniform. With his towering height, he cut an impressive figure among the other delegates.

To Martha he wrote of his sadness at being away from her. But he felt that the war would not last long and that he would be home within months. He would actually be away for six long years.

THE FIRST YEAR OF STRUGGLE: 1775

On June 17, two days after Washington's appointment, fighting exploded in Boston. It was triggered by General Gage, who had now received his requested 4,500 men. He had long wanted to fortify two points, Breed's Hill and Bunker Hill, which loomed across the Charles River and gave a commanding view of the city. The colonists, when surrounding Boston, had left the hills unoccupied. If they now fell into his hands, the colonists would be easy targets for his artillery.

Early that day 2,500 men in skiffs crossed the Charles River, only to find that the colonists had somehow learned of Gage's plan and had moved 1,500 men to the summit of Breed's Hill during the night. Now they stood ready to defend the hill for as long as possible.

The attackers made fine targets as they landed and began to mount the hillside. The colonists waited silently as the wave of red flowed toward them. Then, when the oncomers were within musket range, gunfire exploded. Clouds of smoke burst all along the colonial line. When they cleared, the hillside was in chaos, with the dead and the wounded sprawled everywhere, and red-coated figures dashing back down to the water's edge.

Despite their terrible losses the British turned and hurled themselves back up the hill, only to be met by another deafening volley. Again they reeled down to the water's edge, regrouped, and once more climbed toward the American line. This time there was no rebel gunfire. The colonists had exhausted their ammunition. They now fought with bayonets and fists until forced to retreat to Bunker Hill and beyond. In so doing they gave the battle its name.

To many the day seemed to mark a colonial defeat. But it was actually a major victory, costing the British more than 1,100 casualties. Colonial casualties totaled about 450.

Soon after Bunker Hill, Washington arrived at his headquarters at Cambridge, near Boston. He spent the next months

British troops and American colonists fought hand-to-hand combat during the Battle of Bunker Hill.

organizing his infant army, all the while awaiting the arrival of the weapons needed for his first strike at the enemy. Consisting of fifty cannons and stores of muskets and powder, the weaponry had been taken from Fort Ticonderoga (a British post alongside Lake Champlain) by a group of Vermont patriots and sent for use in a failed invasion of Canada. Then it was brought to Boston, arriving in March 1776.

Immediately Washington moved the weapons to the crest of Dorchester Heights, a string of hills overlooking the city. Then he gave General William Howe, the new British commander at Boston, a harsh choice: either leave or suffer an artillery barrage that would level the city. Howe replied by sailing his men north along the Atlantic coastline to Canada's Nova Scotia.

1776

But as Washington soon learned, General Howe was far from done with him. Word arrived in mid-1776 that Howe was returning with 32,000 troops, sailing down from Nova Scotia to capture New York City. He would then thrust inland to join a redcoat force that was marching in from Canada. Together they would forge a line that would separate Massachusetts from its fellow colonies to the south. The division would render each side too weak to continue fighting by itself. The plan eventually failed when the troops from Canada met a small colonial force led by General Benedict Arnold and were sent home.

Washington replied to the enemy's plan by shifting nine thousand of his troops from Boston to New York City, landing them on Manhattan Island and neighboring Long Island. On Long Island most settled in Brooklyn Heights, overlooking New York City itself.

A DECLARATION OF INDEPENDENCE

Throughout the early months of this same year, while Washington was fighting for America's freedom on the battlefield, an equally daunting effort was being made by the nation's young central government.

The feeling continued to grow among both the public and the members of the Continental Congress that the colonies should at last separate from England. Then, in June, delegate Richard Henry Lee of Virginia offered a resolution in the Congress that "these United Colonies are, and of right ought to be, free and independent states."

John Adams of Massachusetts seconded the resolution. A committee headed by Virginia's Thomas Jefferson was named to draw up an official Declaration of Independence. Appointed to the task with Jefferson were Benjamin Franklin (Pennsylvania), John Adams, Roger Sherman (Connecticut), and Robert R. Livingston (New York).

The Continental Congress voted in favor of declaring formal independence on July 2, 1776. Then, two days later, on a blistering-hot July 4, the written document came before the delegates for debate and adoption.

What they received was principally the work of Thomas Jefferson. It contained an extensive list of oppressive acts charged against King George and went on to assert that "all men are created equal," that all have the right to "life, liberty, and the pursuit of happiness," that governments are established to secure these rights, that the right to rule is derived "from the consent of the governed," and that when a government ceases to guarantee these rights, the people should either alter it or abolish it and then create one that will.

Throughout that unforgettable day, the delegates discussed the declaration, revising phrases and sentences, discarding some, accepting others, and at last reshaping the document so that it met with the approval of its signers and would end with these words:

And for the support of this Declaration, with a firm reliance on the protection of Divine Providence, we mutually pledge to each other our lives, our fortunes, and our sacred Honour.

Printing shops eagerly began turning out hundreds of copies, which were then handed to riders and stuffed into saddlebags for gallops to every colony. Noisy celebrations followed everywhere—on farms, in mountain cabins, in villages, and in the largest of the

Crowds gather outside Independence Hall in Philadelphia as the Declaration of Independence is read aloud.

new nation's cities. The declaration was pinned to bulletin boards, read aloud at public gatherings, and given to soldiers in their encampments.

But with all this joy there was also sorrow. Many colonists had hoped that there would be reconciliation with the mother country and that the ties of old could somehow remain intact. But now such hopefuls, as one colonist wrote, could only recall, "In truth, I wept that day."

GENERAL HOWE'S CRITICAL ERROR

In August, General Howe's 32,000-man army arrived in the New York area aboard a fleet of warships and transports. He quickly attacked the colonists at Brooklyn Heights. The colonists fought stubbornly for hours but were finally overwhelmed by the enemy mass and forced to flee at sunset.

Howe made a critical error at this point. Had he pursued Washington, he might have ended the fighting and perhaps the revolution itself. But he decided to rest his men for a day or two instead. The delay enabled Washington to save his battered army by escaping to New York City on a foggy night.

Washington quickly realized that his men were too raw and untrained to face the enemy in open battle. He decided on a strategy that was to serve him well in the Revolution's early years. It was the strategy of flight.

With the strategy of flight in mind, Washington now left New York City and raced north along the Hudson River, with the

General Washington directed his troops from Long Island to New York City while General Howe's troops rested.

THE STRATEGY OF FLIGHT

From his years with the militia General Washington knew that his soldiers would be courageous, superb marksmen, and physically rugged fighters accustomed to hardship. But he also knew that they would be missing an essential skill. No matter how courageous they may be, they were not trained for warfare, not accustomed to obeying orders instantly, and not accustomed to moving swiftly as if they were one man, putting them at a terrible disadvantage when facing the experienced and well-trained British redcoats.

Something had to be done to even the score. That something, Washington decided, was to keep his men out of battle and out of the enemy's reach for as long as possible—until they had been trained to be efficient soldiers. Or until, and he felt this was vital, the British became so tired that they gave up the war and left the colonies to the colonists.

His decision to avoid battle at first alarmed and angered his fellow officers, earning pleas from them for a change of mind. They all felt that no war could be won except through battle. Nevertheless, only on a few occasions did he abandon his strategy, usually doing so when he thought that battle was necessary. The battles, however, produced mixed results: triumphs at New Jersey's Trenton and Princeton as 1776 turned to 1777; defeat at Pennsylvania's Brandywine Creek in September 1777; victory at Saratoga, New York, a month later; and the 1778 draw at Monmouth, New Jersey.

This well-known painting, Washington Crossing the Delaware, *was painted by Emanuel Gottlieb Leutze. It depicts Washington's flight into Pennsylvania.*

British snapping at his heels. Twice they caught him, defeating him in battle but failing to stop his flight. Finally, in early December 1776, he left New York State behind, crossed into New Jersey, and set out for Pennsylvania.

Throughout much of the chase the British were led by a new commander, General Charles Cornwallis. At last, with Cornwallis only a few miles behind, the colonial flight ended. As winter arrived, Washington reached the Delaware River and sent his men over to its west bank, in Pennsylvania. They made the crossing aboard small boats that they found along the riverbanks, first destroying every boat they didn't need. When Cornwallis reached the Delaware, he found himself stranded on its east bank in New Jersey, with no transport to take him across.

But Cornwallis was not troubled. Winter was at hand. There would be no fighting for weeks to come. His redcoats would rest and then attend to the rebels when spring arrived.

VICTORIES FOR WASHINGTON: 1776–1777

On the other side Washington was deeply worried. His soldiers were sick of fleeing and being away from their families. Their period of enlistment was due to end on December 31, 1776. He felt certain they would refuse to reenlist and would hurry home to help their loved ones survive the harsh winter.

Despite the strategy of flight something had to be done to rekindle their desire to fight. Washington knew there was but one answer. He had to lead them in a successful attack that would keep their spirits alive through the frozen months ahead.

But where should he strike? A glance across the Delaware gave him the answer: the New Jersey town of Trenton. A victory there would do more than lift the spirits of his men. It would inspire them because the town was held by Hessian troops, professional soldiers from Germany. Hired by King George, they numbered 30,000 and had been obtained from Hesse, a German province. They were hated everywhere for their cruelty and thievery.

Washington quickly planned a dawn strike for the day after Christmas. His troops would cross the river in three units and attack together, hoping that the Hessians, after hours of celebrating, would be too tired to mount a strong defense.

Though the plan was a good one, the weather prevented its execution. Snow lashed the colonists as they began the river crossing and turned two of the units back. Only the group led by Washington himself reached the opposite shore, 9 miles north of Trenton.

Matters improved, however, at 8:00 A.M., when his nearly frozen men caught the enemy asleep at Trenton. The few Hessians on sentry duty were quickly subdued. Then, as the sleeping

George Washington leads his men on the early-morning attack against the Hessians in New Jersey.

troops struggled to come awake, the attackers crashed through the town. Trenton was in their hands within ninety minutes, along with several tons of supplies.

The victory delighted the colonists. It was exactly what they needed to rekindle their fighting spirit. Then, suddenly, there was the chance for another victory. They received word that Cornwallis was marching on Trenton with five thousand men and had left seven hundred men camped at nearby Princeton. That village would be the next colonial target.

Cornwallis reached Trenton on January 2, 1777, while the Americans were still camped nearby. But he was stunned the next morning to find them gone. On Washington's orders, they had lighted campfires the previous night as if ready to bed down. Then they had slipped away in the darkness and had marched to Princeton.

There, striking at dawn, they swiftly overcame its redcoat guards. Elated by their second triumph in eight days, they then marched into Pennsylvania and made their way to the village of Morristown, where they settled into their winter quarters to rest until May 1777.

1777

The British decided on a plan for 1777 that resembled the failed 1776 campaign. This time, however, New York State would replace Massachusetts as the target, but the goal would be the same as before: the northern and southern colonies were to be split apart.

Three armies were assigned to the task and were to converge on the city of Albany in New York. Two of their number were to march south from Canada, but both were defeated in battle and fled back across the border. The third force, commanded by General Howe, was to thrust north from New York City.

But for some unknown reason, Howe never received orders from England to join the troops from Canada. As a result he alone decided on his next move. He chose to capture Philadelphia, the home of the Continental Congress. It was a choice that brought him face to face with Washington.

Howe first moved against Philadelphia by marching across New Jersey, but constant skirmishes with Washington turned him back. Next, he sailed down the Atlantic coast with 15,000 troops and entered Chesapeake Bay, which flows north through Virginia and Maryland. On continuing to its northern end, he went ashore near the Pennsylvania border and began a 57-mile hike to Philadelphia.

In August, Washington stepped into Howe's path to meet him at Brandywine Creek. After placing 12,000 men along the creek, he waited to strike as Howe approached, only to be humiliated when a contingent of redcoats stole behind his lines and sent his men running. From there Howe marched to Philadelphia, with the Congress fleeing just before his arrival on September 26, 1777.

Unable to save Philadelphia, Washington quickly chose another target—the nearby village of Germantown, where the British had stationed a large force. Like Trenton in 1776, Germantown offered him the chance of a major victory. It was a chance that he took in a dawn attack on October 4. At first he sent the British scurrying. But when victory seemed in hand, a nightmarish incident snatched it away.

The battle was being fought in a dense fog, and when two of his units blindly stumbled into each other, they began exchanging deadly fire. Before the error was corrected, the British had rallied, and Washington was driven back in full retreat.

As 1777 neared its end, Washington and Howe moved into winter quarters, with Washington settling at Valley Forge, Pennsylvania. There, the colonists faced the cruelest months of the war.

NIGHTMARE AT VALLEY FORGE

While the British were housed in comfort in Philadelphia, the colonial troops lived in squalid cabins that they had built themselves. In one of the most severe winters in years, they were poorly clothed and fed (in great part because many companies, fearing that the infant United States would be unable to pay for its purchases, refused to extend credit to the army).

As a result more than three thousand of the Valley Forge soldiers had no shoes. They tried to protect their feet by binding them in blanket strips, but to little avail. Among the most familiar sights at the camp that year were bloody footprints left in the snow.

Though their suffering was great, the men managed to survive the freezing months, gathering what little food they could

General Washington and the Marquis de Lafayette among the troops at Valley Forge.

find in the surrounding countryside and then fishing the nearby streams when the warming weather caused the ice to thaw.

Despite these countless hardships, some good news arrived. Several aristocratic Europeans with military backgrounds—among them France's Marquis de Lafayette and Germany's Baron Friedrich von Steuben—had joined the new nation's bid for independence and now worked to turn the colonial troops into effective soldiers through intense drills and lessons in military discipline. By spring they had done much to transform their pupils into well-trained and disciplined fighters.

Washington established his Valley Forge headquarters in a stone farmhouse on the banks of the Schuylkill River. On taking over the house, he ordered that an extra dining room be built so that he could accommodate larger groups of his officers for meetings and dinners.

Martha Washington also went to Valley Forge and brought much comfort to the sick and wounded. Often carrying a basket of food tidbits, she left the farmhouse that she shared with her husband and toured the camp, chatting with the soldiers, and distributing morsels of food as she went. The superb leadership displayed by both Martha and her husband would contribute to the boundless affection the nation would eventually pour on them when the time came to chose its first formal leader, and that time would arrive sooner rather than later.

The Tide Turns: 1778–1781

Early in 1778 good news arrived from across the Atlantic. Urged by Benjamin Franklin, France recognized the independence of the United States and began to provide military and financial aid. Franklin, who was now in his seventies, had gone to Paris as a representative of the new nation. There he secured more than $2 million in financial support, plus the assignment of French warships and troops to further the U.S. cause. France would soon be joined by Spain and Holland, in 1779 and 1780, respectively, in backing the U.S. cause.

In 1778 the British government ordered its troops to abandon Philadelphia so that they could fortify other points against possible French attacks. In addition, after the failures in Massachusetts and New York, London decided to forget the northern states and strike at those in the South.

The struggle for the South began in December 1778, when British warships struck the South Carolina coast and captured the city of Charleston. Troops commanded by General Cornwallis set out to take both Carolinas, only to meet stubborn resistance wherever they went. Patriot fighters under such leaders as Francis

Marion and Thomas Sumter constantly fired on his scouting parties and destroyed his supply wagons. Their small-scale raids eventually forced Cornwallis to make two stands on the border dividing the Carolinas. In both encounters he was soundly defeated.

THE FINAL BATTLE

Beginning in 1780 life changed greatly for Washington. First, fighting the battles themselves shifted to other generals, among them Nathanael Greene, the commander of the American forces in the South. This left Washington free to deal with such vital matters as army finance and the placement of the steadily mounting number of French troops.

Second, in 1781 the revolution turned permanently in the favor of the Americans. General Greene's troops, joined by guerrilla fighters under Francis Marion and Thomas Sumter, struck hard at Cornwallis and drove him north through the Carolinas. On entering Virginia, he came upon Americans serving with one of the great heroes of Valley Forge, the Marquis de Lafayette. Though known for his courage, the French nobleman steadily retreated before the enemy because he desperately needed reinforcements.

Then, suddenly, Lafayette ended his flight when the needed reinforcements arrived. He not only stopped running but now began to menace Cornwallis. Alarmed, the Englishman entered the port town of Yorktown, on a cape extending into Chesapeake Bay. Here, his troops, seven thousand in all, dug in to wait for help that was expected from Britain.

Washington was with troops 300 miles to the north when word about Yorktown reached him. Astonished, he saw that Cornwallis had placed himself in a pocket with water on three sides, a deadly trap should U.S. and French ships close in on it. He quickly raced south to join Lafayette for a final assault on the enemy. Altogether he had 16,000 U.S. and French troops on the move.

By the time all of Washington's troops arrived at Yorktown in early October, the port was alive with warships. But they were not British vessels meant to sail Cornwallis to safety and the chance to fight another day. Rather, riding at anchor were twenty-eight French warships that had come north from the West Indies.

Cornwallis realized that he had placed himself in an

Washington arrived at Yorktown to battle Cornwallis in the final battle of the Revolution.

impossible situation. He had counted on being rescued from the sea. But now, with enemy ships crowding all around, he knew there would be no such rescue.

Though caught in a trap, Cornwallis remained in place for more than a week. Throughout those days the cannons of the French ships and the rebel land forces shelled him constantly. At last he accepted what he had always known, that he had no choice but to surrender.

The surrender came on October 19, 1781. The war would end formally in 1783 with the signing of a peace treaty in Paris. The October surrender, however, marked the close of most of the fighting. At last the United States of America stood victorious as an independent nation.

By November 1783 all but a few British troops had left the United States, with some returning home and others moving to posts in Canada and elsewhere. In December, George Washington said a quiet farewell to his officers and retired from the army. At age fifty-one he returned to Martha and Mount Vernon to begin life anew.

It was a life much like the one of his earlier years. He checked his fields daily, pursued his agricultural experiments, and embarked on a building program that would provide Mount Vernon with new chimneys, a banquet hall, and a mill.

As he was renewing his life in Virginia, national events were taking shape that would affect George Washington's and his country's future. They would shoulder him with duties even more demanding than those he had borne during the Revolution.

A Second New Document for the Nation

Between 1777 and 1781 the members of the Second Continental Congress enacted what were called the Articles of Confederation. The Articles established a government that gave the Continental Congress the power to raise an army and to wage war, if necessary. But they did not provide the country with the strength it needed to govern itself. They established a central government that consisted only of a congress that was merely an advisory body to the states. It could make laws, but it had no power to enforce them. It could request funds from the states for projects meant for the national good, but it had no power to collect them. It had no control over the trade conducted between the states and with foreign nations.

The result was that quarrels constantly erupted among the states over commerce, taxation, public funds, and state boundaries. These were the problems of states that had always handled their own affairs and knew little about cooperating with each other.

In May 1787, deeply worried about such problems, the state leaders set about correcting the weaknesses in the Articles. Meeting in Philadelphia's Independence Hall for what they called a Constitutional Convention were fifty-five representatives from twelve of the thirteen states (absent was Rhode Island, due to the fear of its citizens that the convention would lead to the government gaining too much power over the people). The delegates included some of the most brilliant men in the country, such as Benjamin Franklin, James Madison, Alexander Hamilton, and once again, George Washington.

Washington, who headed the Virginia delegation, was unanimously elected as the convention's presiding officer and quietly watched over the delegates during the four months they spent fashioning a constitution for the nation. It was a document that would give the new United States a government completely different from any that had existed previously. It called for the formation of three branches of

George Washington presided over the Constitutional Convention in Philadelphia in 1787.

government: a legislative branch consisting of two houses (the Senate and the House of Representatives), an executive branch headed by the president, and a judicial branch composed of the Supreme Court and several lesser courts. To prevent any branch from gaining too much strength, each was given powers that restricted those of the others. As a result the U.S. government became known as a government of checks and balances.

Once it was approved by the delegates, the proposed constitution faced a critical test. It was placed before the state governments for approval or rejection. Nine of the thirteen states had to vote in its favor before it could become the law of the land.

One by one, after months of heated debate over points in the document, nine states voted to accept the Constitution of the United States. In the order of their approval they were Delaware, Pennsylvania, New Jersey, Georgia, Connecticut, Massachusetts, Maryland, South Carolina, and New Hampshire, with the New Hampshire vote coming on June 1, 1788. Thereafter, Virginia, New York, North Carolina, and Rhode Island gave their approval. During the next three years the newborn document was amended ten times to provide the nation's four million citizens with a statement of their individual rights, among them the freedoms of speech, the press, and religion. These ten amendments soon became known as the Bill of Rights.

AMERICA'S FIRST PRESIDENT

Once the Constitution was approved, the state legislatures set about electing the nation's first president. He was to be chosen not by popular vote but, as specified in the Constitution, by means of the electoral college. The results were then to remain secret until the new Congress met in 1789 in New York City, which had been chosen as the seat of the infant government.

When the ballots were finally opened on April 6 of that year, they revealed that every state had named George Washington to the presidency.

His selection came as no surprise to the country. Adding to the prestige won during the Revolution was the respect he had earned with his quiet leadership while the Continental Congress was shaping the Constitution. It was also widely known that he was not a man so driven by political ambitions that he would become a public danger; after all, he had voluntarily given up his dictatorial military powers at the close of the Revolution. He was deeply trusted by Americans everywhere.

Washington, however, greeted his victory with mixed feelings. He was now fifty-seven years old and was at last enjoying life at Mount Vernon. Further, despite the work he had already done for the nation, he felt that he did not possess the political abilities and skills necessary to be an effective president. For one, he recognized that he was not an inspiring public speaker and thus lacked one of the basic requirements for political success. For another, he was a member of Virginia's upper class, a position that could harm him in the eyes of many. His lifestyle seemed at odds with that expected of the president of a nation of the people.

Further, he knew that Martha hated the thought of the problems that the coming years would place on his aging shoulders. He shared her concerns about his health. He suffered from rheumatism and severe colds. He had lost his teeth, a loss that caused him to wear dentures that were uncomfortable and, at times, painful. They were carved from the ivory of hippopotamus teeth; added to them was one of his own teeth.

But Washington felt that he could not ignore the honor that the nation was according him. And so on April 16, 1789, he left Mount Vernon and set out for New York City. Just before departing, he expressed his feelings in a good-humored letter to his longtime friend Henry Knox: "[M]y movements to the chair at government will be accompanied by feelings not unlike those of a culprit, who is going to the place of his execution."

Throughout the eight-day journey northward he was greeted by admiring crowds—20,000 people in Philadelphia alone—roaring cannons, banquets, and speeches. The journey ended in late April, when he stood on a balcony at Federal Hall

President-elect George Washington is greeted warmly on his route to his inauguration in New York.

overlooking Wall Street and took his oath of office. Standing with him in front of several thousand spectators and taking the oath of vice president was the diminutive and stout John Adams, who would become the nation's second president.

New Homes for a New Job

As Washington set about acquainting himself with his new job, Martha began to establish a home for the family in New York, settling them in a brick house on Cherry Street, with Washington choosing an office for himself on the third floor. The home was spacious, but its roominess was severely challenged when the couple moved in with Martha's two grandchildren and a staff of eighteen servants.

The family, however, remained at the Cherry Street address until 1790. At that time plans were approved to move the nation's capital to Virginia and to build a city for it there. First called Federal City, it was to stand near Mount Vernon and, in time, would be renamed Washington, D.C. While Federal City was under construction, the federal government settled temporarily in Philadelphia, with the Washingtons moving into a home that George happily called "the best single house in the city."

The New York and Philadelphia homes were constantly crowded with visitors, guests attending state dinners, dignitaries attending social gatherings, and an unending daily parade of people calling for business and political reasons. Of that unending parade Washington once complained:

I could not get relieved from the ceremony of one visit, before I had to attend to another. . . . I had no leisure to read or to answer the dispatches that were pouring in upon me from all quarters.

George and Martha cooperated in scheduling social events so that they interfered with his work as little as possible. For example, Tuesday afternoons were set aside for dignitaries and others who wished to meet the president. On arriving, the guests were introduced to Washington as he stood in front of the living-room fireplace, after which they gathered in a large circle. He then moved slowly from guest to guest, speaking a few words to each. The afternoon ended when he returned to the fireplace for a final bow from each departing guest.

Evenings were also set aside at times for smaller gatherings, both formal and informal. To these were invited colleagues, distinguished visitors, and old friends. Both men and women were welcome, except on Friday nights, which were reserved for men only.

President and Mrs. Washington receive guests at a presidential reception.

No matter the evening occasion, Martha established a custom that would last throughout George's presidency. When the clock chimed nine, she would rise and graciously bid the guests good night with the announcement, "Mr. Washington and I retire at 9 o'clock."

Their homes were to bother Washington throughout his presidency. Spacious though they were, he always thought them too modest to put the U.S. president on an equal footing with other heads of state. To help offset that problem, he always carried himself with great dignity, dressing in black during formal occasions and displaying a sword beneath his coat. Far more ornate was the gold-trimmed saddle worn by his white horse, and most ornate of all was the carriage in which he rode. Pulled by four, or at times six, handsome bays, it was painted a cream color and was attended by a driver and coachmen decked out in scarlet livery.

In his public dress and manner Washington constantly sought to impress and win the respect of foreign nations. But at the same time he disliked the pomp that was always on view among the European nobility, preferring simple ceremonies instead. He reacted angrily on hearing someone address him as "Your Highness" and ordered that the term never be used again. He shook his head when Vice President John Adams recommended that he be addressed as "His Most Benign Highness."

Washington himself preferred the simplest of the forms of address suggested for his use, "Mr. President." Adams disputed the choice, saying that it could be used to designate the head of any small organization, even a sports group. But Washington's preference eventually replaced all other forms of address, and the simple and direct "Mr. President" has remained to this day.

WASHINGTON HELPS A NATION TAKE SHAPE

Six

While the family was settling itself on Cherry Street in New York, Washington faced his first task as president, the appointment of the three men who would serve as his chief advisers. They would constitute the beginnings of what came to be called his cabinet. Selected were Secretary of State Thomas Jefferson, Secretary of the Treasury Alexander Hamilton, and Secretary of War Henry Knox. Appointed also was Edmund Randolph as attorney general. His was not a cabinet position, but he was invited to attend all meetings of the group.

In addition to these appointments Washington spent long hours selecting the men who would fill a host of federal jobs, among them inspectors of foreign goods entering U.S. ports, collectors of federal revenue, district attorneys, and federal judges. Of the

The men selected for the first presidential Cabinet were Henry Knox, Thomas Jefferson, Alexander Hamilton, and Edmund Randolph (left to right).

several hundred applicants for court positions thirty-five were considered for appointment to the country's highest court, the Supreme Court. Six were finally selected for positions on the court, with one of their number, John Jay of New York, being named the court's first chief justice.

Financing the New Nation

The nation immediately set about raising the funds needed for its support. Heading this work was Secretary of the Treasury Alexander Hamilton. While in the midst of organizing the treasury department, he successfully urged Congress to approve several tariffs and taxes that would help put the United States on a sound financial footing. Next, he pressed Congress to improve the country's credit both at home and overseas.

To accomplish this, he proposed that the federal government pay off *all* U.S. debts, a total of about $12 million owed to foreign nations, chiefly France, Spain, and Holland. At the same time he called for the federal government to take over the state debts of $42 million.

For long months the plan triggered heated arguments in homes, offices, and taverns throughout the country. Much of the trouble centered on the idea of having the federal government take over the state's debts. States with small debts objected to the idea of sharing in the payments of states heavily in debt. In time Hamilton's plan won congressional approval. The debts of both the nation and the states were assumed and paid by the federal government.

Once the idea of paying the nation's debts was launched, Hamilton persuaded Congress to establish the country's first national bank, to be housed in Philadelphia and called the Bank

Workers in the pressing and culling room of the United States Mint in Philadelphia.

of the United States. At first the idea was severely criticized, with the bank's opponents claiming that it would become a government monopoly by providing unfair competition for private banks. In the dispute Washington sided with Hamilton, gave the proposed bank his support, and saw it open for business in 1791.

A year later another Hamilton project took shape, the formation of the United States Mint in Philadelphia. Washington knew this would be a necessary component of the nation. The infant mint began producing money that could be used everywhere, ending the old practice of each state producing its own money that might or might not be accepted for use elsewhere. That the United States now had its own national currency did much to encourage the growth of interstate trade and commerce.

Two Political Parties

During Washington's first term, the country witnessed the birth of two political parties, the Federalist Party and the Democratic-Republican Party.

The Federalists, who favored a strong central government, were led by Alexander Hamilton and included Washington among their admirers. In the Federalist camp were the best-educated and wealthiest of the nation's people. They believed that a proper government was one in which trained political leaders handled the important affairs of the nation, with less important matters being left to state, county, and town governments. In such a government some power was taken from the common people but was given to those thought best suited to govern.

The Democratic-Republicans, headed by Thomas Jefferson, wanted the national government kept firmly in the hands of the people and never surrendered to a potentially dictatorial ruler. Many farmers and people living in small towns supported this idea, hating the thought of any power slipping away from ordinary folks and passing into the hands of those in the nation's capital.

Though the two parties were widely supported, neither had a candidate strong enough to challenge Washington when the presidential election of 1792 was held. Friends and family knew that Washington ached to return to Mount Vernon but was hesitant to do so. One of his greatest fears was that his departure would severely weaken public support for the Bank of the United States, leading to the collapse of the bank and perhaps even the collapse of the Union. He had to remain in office to give the bank the backing it needed.

With that aim in mind he was unanimously elected in 1792, at age sixty, to his second term as the nation's president.

THE SECOND TERM

Another of Alexander Hamilton's projects, a tax on alcoholic liquors, caused trouble for Washington soon after the start of his second term. The trouble began when Congress enacted the tax and angered the many backwoods farmers who grew large quantities of corn (which was necessary for the manufacture of many liquors) for sale. They had always found it difficult to haul their corn to market over the rough trails of the day and for years had been making the trips easier by distilling the corn into liquor for transport.

The liquor tax bit deeply into their profits, and it angered the growers in Pennsylvania so much that they rebelled in 1794. They refused to pay the tax and severely beat the government agents sent to collect it. Washington, realizing that the laws of the nation had always to be respected, quickly dispatched 13,000 militia troops to subdue what was soon being called the Whiskey Rebellion. Upon the troops' arrival, the revolt collapsed.

PROBLEMS OVERSEAS

The Whiskey Rebellion was but a minor issue for Washington in comparison to a great challenge from Europe. In 1789, shortly after Washington's first term as president began, the French people rid their nation of its long-standing rule by kings. In its place they established a republican government, an action that led them to war with England. Along with other nations throughout Europe, the British feared that a similar rebellion would overthrow their own king and government.

Secretary of State Thomas Jefferson and many other Americans approved of the new French republican government and wanted to support it politically and financially. Washington, however, angered them in 1793 by holding firmly to a national policy of neutrality—basically, of not taking a side on the issue. In so doing he also upset both the British and the French. England argued that most Americans were of English descent and, regardless of the Revolutionary War, should support the former mother country. The French, on the other hand, felt that America should side with them because of the help they gave during the Revolution. But Washington would not budge, as he decided his young nation had been through enough conflict.

Washington's insistence on remaining neutral was threatened when an angry Britain began attacking American merchant vessels and impressing their crews into service aboard British ships in the war with France. In 1795, seeking to end this problem, Washington sent Chief Justice John Jay to England to arrange a treaty that would stop the British attacks. Though the pact failed to achieve its primary goal, it did put an end to another long-standing problem, as the British agreed to give up a number of forts in western America they had held since the Revolutionary War.

Because of America's neutral stance on the issue with France and England, British vessels began to impress American seamen.

The terms were disappointing, but Washington urged the acceptance of the treaty in 1795, saying that it was the best that could be had at the moment. For most Americans, though, its terms were more than disappointing; they were galling. All that the agreement promised was the removal of redcoat troops that the British had already said they would remove at war's end—in other words the treaty was not giving the Americans anything they didn't already have. A wave of anger rolled through the country. Jay was taunted in the streets. Jeers and rocks greeted Hamilton when he spoke in favor of the treaty. Jefferson joined the outcry against the pact, calling it a surrender to the British. Before the anger finally subsided, Washington remarked that he would rather be in his grave than in his present situation.

THE FINAL YEARS

The year 1796 was eagerly anticipated by George Washington. It brought the nation's next presidential election and the beginning of his retirement. He was determined to return to private life and declared that he would not serve a third term as president.

In his decision Washington set a tradition that was to continue until the mid-twentieth century. It was then that Franklin D. Roosevelt, to see the completion of his leadership in World War II, won the presidency for a third time. The Washington tradition, however, was formally reinstated in 1951 by the Twenty-second Amendment to the Constitution.

Washington's decision to depart became public when a lengthy article, bearing his name and called "the Farewell Address," appeared in the nation's newspapers. The address had three parts: his plea that the people work hard for national unity, his review of the nation's problems, and his advice that Americans avoid permanent foreign alliances. In a text originally written for him by James Madison (who would become the nation's fourth president) and revised by Alexander Hamilton, he held that

The great rule of conduct for us, in regard to foreign nations, is, in extending our commercial relations, to have with them as little political connection as possible. So far as we have already formed engagements, let them be fulfilled with perfect good faith. Here let us stop.

It was advice that proved impossible to follow through the years, as the world grew smaller and warfare became a greater threat than ever through the increasing speed of modern communications.

When Washington finally returned to Virginia at age sixty-four, he was one of the most revered men in the nation, though some of the problems that he faced during his presidency—among them his insistence on remaining neutral in the troubles between England and France—had earned him many political enemies. For the most part, however, he was viewed in a positive light.

Settled once more at Mount Vernon, Washington began the final two-and-a-half years of his life. They were filled with the daily care of the estate. He also personally selected the site for the planned national capital, which was to be located on lands ceded to the federal government by Maryland and Virginia (with the Virginia property eventually being returned to the state). Finally, he agreed to command the army in 1798, when a war with France loomed briefly on the horizon, but happily for him, he was never called to perform this duty.

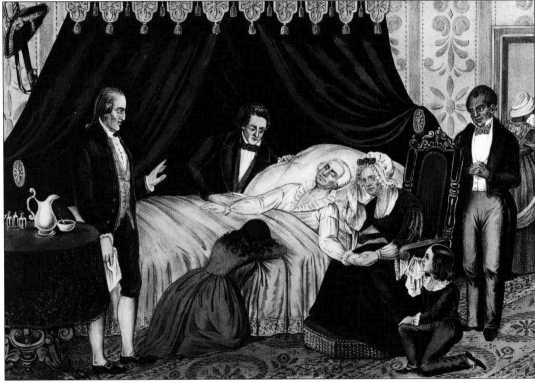

Family and friends surround Washington at the time of his death, in 1799.

Washington spent his final weeks at home, in 1799, with death coming at year's end. He went riding to inspect his property on a stormy December 12, becoming ill with a sore throat. His condition steadily worsened as doctors, employing one of the era's most widely used treatments, bled and purged him. Finally, on the night of December 14, he told his doctors, "I thank you for your attentions, but I pray you to take no more trouble with me." At the age of sixty-seven George Washington died quietly just before midnight.

During his remarkable lifetime Washington played a pivotal role in helping America gain its much-needed freedom from

Parson Weems and the Birth of a Legend

During the decades since his death George Washington has been the subject of many biographies for both adults and young people. One of the best remembered is a work titled *Life of George Washington*.

The reason the book, which was written sometime around 1800 by Mason L. Weems, is so well remembered is not that it is a fine biography that tells us much about the man and his work. Rather, it is remembered for the fairy-tale stories that Weems invented for it.

The best known of their number is the tale of young George and the cherry tree. When George's father discovered that someone had felled the slender tree with an ax, he asked the boy if he was the one responsible for the damage. George quickly replied that he could not tell a lie and that yes, he had done it.

Weems invented the story in part to make his book interesting and in part to create a heroic figure. He felt that the people of the new United States needed heroes to give them great pride in their nation. Today he has the reputation of having created a president who was simply too good to be true.

Weems, who bore the nickname "Parson," was a clergyman who made his living as a door-to-door book peddler. He wrote the Washington book to add to his income and then saw it earn more money than he had ever imagined. It was printed in more than seventy editions. Among them were five editions in German.

unjust colonial rule and in forming a stable central government. All in all it is doubtful that America would have been able to sustain its independence and find the road ahead without him. He created the foundation on which the United States could build a glorious and storied future. He was, as legend proclaims, the father of the nation.

Leaving Martha, who would live until 1802, behind, George Washington was buried at Mount Vernon. Memorials in his honor followed throughout the country, including in Congress. In the House of Representatives the members passed a resolution written by Henry Lee, who had served under Washington in the Revolution as a cavalry officer. It closed with the words by which the nation has long remembered one of its most towering figures: "first in war, first in peace, and first in the hearts of his countrymen."

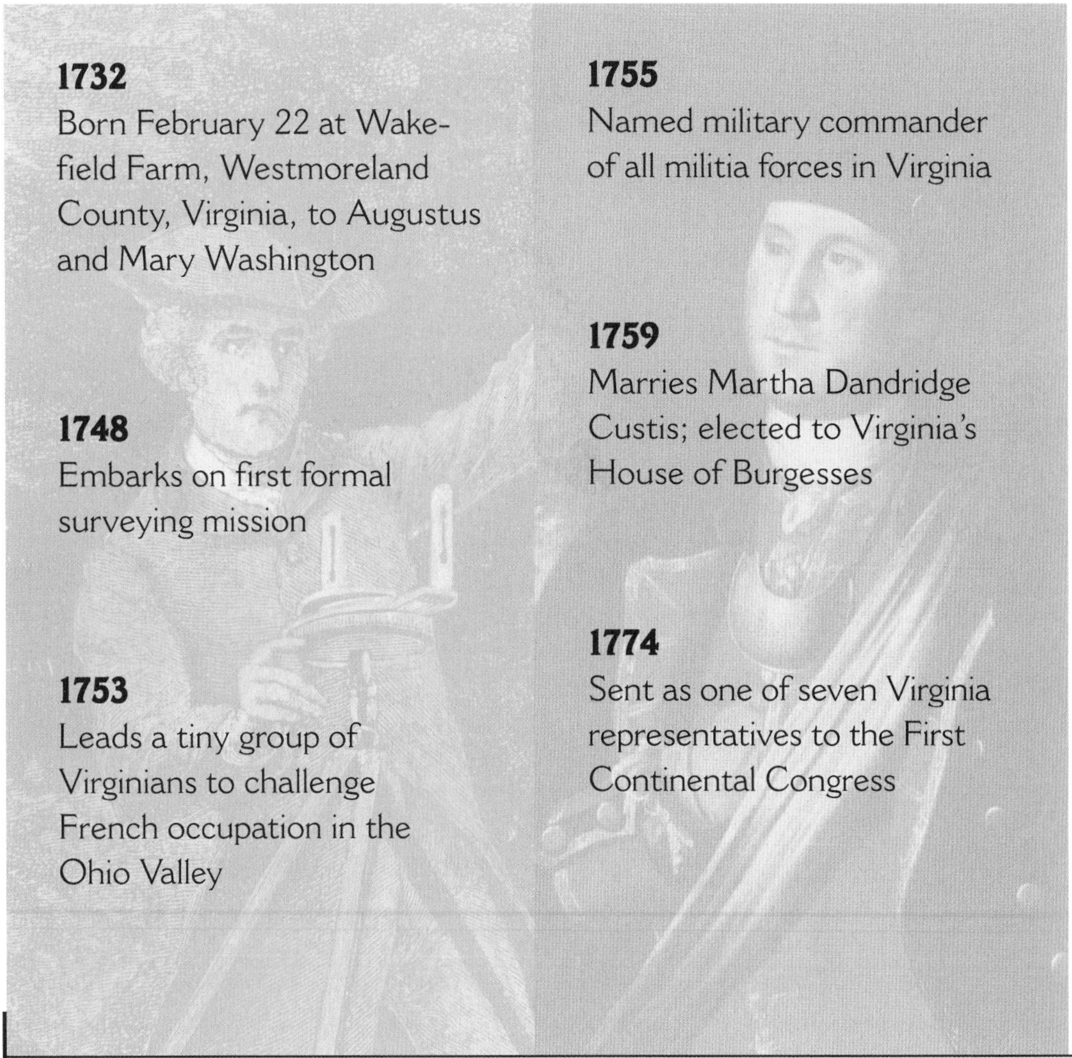

1732

Born February 22 at Wakefield Farm, Westmoreland County, Virginia, to Augustus and Mary Washington

1748

Embarks on first formal surveying mission

1753

Leads a tiny group of Virginians to challenge French occupation in the Ohio Valley

1755

Named military commander of all militia forces in Virginia

1759

Marries Martha Dandridge Custis; elected to Virginia's House of Burgesses

1774

Sent as one of seven Virginia representatives to the First Continental Congress

1730

1775
Attends the meeting of the Second Continental Congress; elected as commander-in-chief of America's forces

1777–1778
Winters at Valley Forge, Pennsylvania, with his troops

1789
Elected the first president of the United States

1792
Elected to second term as president

1796
Finishes second term as president and writes famous "Farewell Address"; returns to Mount Vernon

1799
Dies December 14 at his Mount Vernon home

1800

Articles of Confederation Precursor to the Constitution of the United States, it established a set of laws and rules that empowered the first formal government of the independent nation.

Bill of Rights The first ten amendments to the Constitution of the United States. They were written to protect American citizens by clearly stating their rights and privileges.

Constitutional Convention The assembly that drafted the Constitution of the United States.

Committees of Correspondence A series of colonial groups that exchanged letters reporting on British actions in various parts of the colonies.

Constitution of the United States Created in 1787 as an improvement on the Articles of Confederation, it is essentially a list of the basic laws and rules that govern the United States of America. It was ratified by the thirteen original states in 1789 and has been amended a number of times in the years since.

Continental Congress A group of elected representatives from each of the colonies that assembled before and during the Revolutionary War to discuss and decide the future of an independent America.

Declaration of Independence A document written in 1776, mostly by Thomas Jefferson, and eventually signed by all members of the Continental Congress, stating America's independence from England, its former colonial master.

Democratic-Republican Party Early American political party that favored rule of the nation by representatives elected by ordinary people, thus keeping the bulk of political power in the hands of the citizens.

electoral college System through which the American president and vice president are chosen, in which each state has a certain number of electoral votes based on the combined number of senators and representatives from that state.

Federalist Party Early American political party that favored rule of the nation by the wealthiest and most-educated people.

Intolerable Acts Five oppressive British laws that were enacted in 1774, after the Boston Tea Party.

militia A group of individuals who perform the duties of soldiers, although they are not formally trained as such. A militia usually consists of ordinary people who are conscripted or volunteer to fight under dire or otherwise unusual circumstances.

Navigation Acts A series of British measures that infuriated the colonists in the years prior to the Revolution.

Peace of Utrecht The 1713 treaty that ended a series of inter-European wars and cost France much of its land in North America.

redcoats Name given to British soldiers during the Revolutionary War, due to the handsome red coats they wore.

surveying The practice of determining and measuring the features of any land-mass (such as length, width, and angularity) through the use of various tools (such as a level and a compass) and the mathematical disciplines of geometry and trigonometry.

tariffs Payments that the colonists had to make to Great Britain for various imported goods, among them clothing and printed materials.

Townshend Acts A series of acts passed in the 1760s that required the colonists to pay taxes on a variety of goods vital to daily life.

Books

Adler, David. *George Washington: An Illustrated Biography*. New York: Holiday House, 2004.

Aronson, Marc. *The Real Revolution: The Global Story of American Independence*. New York: Clarion Books, 2005.

Ellis, Joseph J. *His Excellency: George Washington*. New York: Alfred A. Knopf, 2004.

Leighton, Marian. *George Washington*. Edina, MN: ABDO Publishing, 2005.

McGowen, Tom. *The Revolutionary War and George Washington's Army in American History*. Berkeley Heights, NJ: Enslow Publishers, 2004.

Videos

A&E Home Video. *George Washington*. 2004.

Paladin Communications. *George Washington's First War: The Battles at Fort Duquesne*. 2003.

Web Sites

Archiving Early America

http://www.earlyamerica.com/
This site includes links, games, and lots of information about early America, particularly the 1700s.

The American Revolution

http://www.kidinfo.com/American_History/American_Revolution.html
Plenty of solid information about the American Revolution, plus links
to hundreds of other sites, can be found on this site.

Mount Vernon

http://www.mountvernon.org
Explore Mount Vernon, the home of George Washington. This site
highlights the estate grounds, the museum collections, and the
preservation and archaeological efforts taking place on the estate.
Links to related Web sites are provided.

Boorstin, Daniel J., with foreword by Sean Wilentz. *The Americans: The National Experience*. New York: The History Book Club by arrangement with Random House, 2002.

Bowman, John. *The History of the American Presidency*, revised edition. North Dighton, MA: World Publications Group, 2002.

Boyer, Paul S., editor. *The Oxford Companion to United States History*. Oxford, England: Oxford University Press, 2001.

Brookhiser, Richard, editor and commentator. *Rules of Civility: The 110 Precepts That Guided Our First President in War and Peace*. New York: The Free Press, a division of Simon & Shuster, 1997.

————. *Founding Father: Rediscovering George Washington*. New York: The Free Press, 1996.

Burns, James MacGregor, and Susan Dunn. *George Washington*. New York: Times Books, Henry Holt, 2004.

Carrison, Daniel J. *George Washington*. New York: Franklin Watts, 1969.

Carruth, Gorton. *The Encyclopedia of American Facts and Dates*, ninth edition. New York: HarperCollins, 1993.

Chambers, John Whiteclay, II, editor. *The Oxford Companion to American Military History*. Oxford, England: Oxford University Press, 1999.

Dolan, Edward F. *The American Revolution: How We Fought the War of Independence*. Brookfield, CT: Millbrook Press, 1995.

Ellis, Joseph J. *Founding Brothers: The Revolutionary Generation*. New York: Alfred A. Knopf, 2000.

———. *His Excellency: George Washington*. New York: Alfred A. Knopf, 2004.

Fleming, Thomas J. *First in Their Hearts: A Biography of George Washington*. New York: Walker, 1968; reissued 1984.

Holmes, Richard, editor. *The Oxford Companion to Military History*. New York: Oxford University Press, 2001.

Marrin, Albert. *George Washington and the Founding of the Nation*. New York: Dutton, 2001.

Morison, Samuel Eliot. *By Land and Sea*. New York: Alfred A. Knopf, 1953.

Osborne, Mary Pope. *George Washington: Leader of a New Nation*. New York: Dial Books for Young Readers, 1991.

Stokesbury, James L. *A Short History of the American Revolution*. New York: William Morrow, 1991.

Washington, George. *George-isms: The 110 Rules George Washington Wrote When He Was 14—and Lived by All His Life*. New York: Atheneum Books for Young Readers, 2000.

Pages in **boldface** are illustrations.

★ ★ ★ ★ ★ ★ ★ ★ ★ ★ ★ ★ ★ ★ ★ ★ ★ ★ ★

Edward F. Dolan is the author of 120 published nonfiction books. Divided between books for young people and books for adults, they range in subject matter from biographies to current events to the history of warfare. A native of California, Mr. Dolan lives near San Francisco.

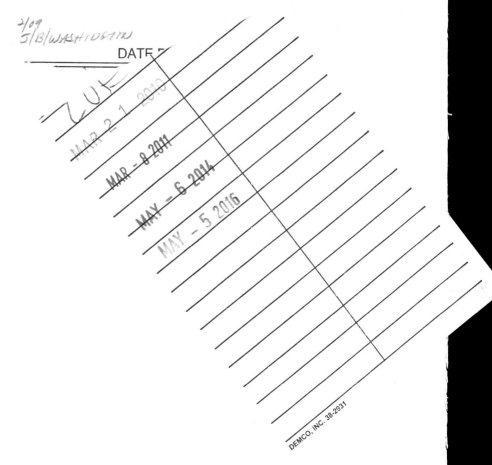

2/09
5/B/WASHINGTON

DATE

MAR 2 1 2010

MAR - 8 2011

MAY - 6 2014

MAY - 5 2016

DEMCO, INC. 38-2931